discovermore

Earth's Processes

What Is the Carbon Cycle?

Doug Bradley

Britannica
Educational Publishing
IN ASSOCIATION WITH
THE ROSEN PUBLISHING GROUP

Published in 2027 by Britannica Educational Publishing (a trademark of Encyclopædia Britannica, Inc.) in association with The Rosen Publishing Group, Inc.
2544 Clinton Street, Buffalo, NY 14224

Distributed exclusively by Rosen Publishing.
To see additional Britannica Educational Publishing titles, go to rosenpublishing.com.

Editor: Greg Roza
Book Design: Deanna Lepovich

Photo Credits: Cover PACO COMO/Shutterstock.com; (series background) Dai Yim/Shutterstock.com; p. 4 EgolenaHK/Shuttersrtock.com; p. 4 (inset) Bjoern Wylezich/Shutterstock.com; p. 5 Nina Buday/Shutterstock.com; p. 7 (top) Nick Dale Photo/Shutterstock.com; p. 7 (bottom) Hryshchyshen Serhii/Shutterstock.com; p. 8 BlueRingMedia/Shutterstock.com; p. 9 Digi.Pixel/Shutterstock.com; p. 10 p.tapenko/Shutterstock.com; p. 11 Jo Dilnot/Shutterstock.com; p. 13 (top) EB Adventure Photography/Shutterstock.com; p. 13 (bottom) rangizzz/Shutterstock.com; p. 14 zombiu26/Shutterstock.com; p. 15 Marina Kryuchina/Shutterstock.com; p. 16 Carl Schoeneich/Shutterstock.com; p. 17 LukaKikina/Shutterstock.com; p. 19 (top) PeopleImages/Shutterstock.com; p. 19 (bottom) Art_Pictures/Shutterstock.com; p. 20 kukurund/Shutterstock.com; p. 21 testing/Shutterstock.com; p. 22 William Edge/Shutterstock.com; p. 23 Lazy_Bear/Shutterstock.com; p. 24 acro_phuket/Shutterstock.com; p. 25 Grinnell Glacier 1938, 1981, 1998, 2005, 2009, 2021/Wikimedia Commons; p. 26 Mozgova/Shutterstock.com; p. 27 Andrey_Popov/Shutterstock.com; p. 28 Mr.Tempter/Shutterstock.com; p. 29 Hryshchyshen Serhii/Shutterstock.com.

Cataloging-in-Publication Data

Names: Bradley, Doug, 1971-.
Title: What is the carbon cycle? / Doug Bradley.
Description: New York : Britannica Educational Publishing, in association with Rosen Educational Services, 2027. | Series: Discover more: Earth's processes | Includes glossary and index.
Identifiers: ISBN 9781641906142 (library bound) | ISBN 9781641906135 (pbk) | ISBN 9781641906159 (ebook)
Subjects: LCSH: Carbon cycle (Biogeochemistry)--Juvenile literature.
Classification: LCC QH344.B656 2027 | DDC 577.144--dc23

Printed in China

CPSIA Compliance Information: Batch #QSBRIT27. For further information contact Rosen Publishing at 1-800-237-9932.

Contents

Carbon Is Everywhere!

Chemical elements are the building blocks for all matter. They are basic substances that cannot be broken down into simpler substances. Carbon is one of the most important chemical elements. Scientists use symbols to stand for the chemical elements.
The symbol for carbon is C.

Pure carbon exists in nature in several forms. Graphite is used to make the leads of pencils. Diamonds are used in jewelry.

All living things are part of the carbon cycle.

On its own, carbon makes up only a small part of Earth's crust. But it combines with other elements very easily to form substances called compounds. Carbon compounds make up 18 percent of all the matter in living things. Living things are all around us. You are a living thing. So are animals and plants. Living things move, grow, and take in chemicals and nutrients.

Carbon is constantly being used and replaced in nature through what is known as the carbon **cycle**. Carbon passes through living things, as well as through Earth's rocks, water, and air. Sometimes it can stay in one place for many years. Other times it moves very quickly.

WORD WISE

A CYCLE IS A SERIES OF EVENTS OR ACTIONS THAT REPEAT REGULARLY.

Stored Carbon

Carbon is found in Earth's hydrosphere (waters), atmosphere (the layer of gases surrounding the planet), lithosphere (rocky outer layer), and biosphere (where life happens). These places are called carbon reservoirs, or places where carbon exists in large amounts.

Without carbon, life as we know it would not exist. All plants and animals are made of tissues. These tissues are built of elements grouped around chains or rings made of carbon atoms.

Living things produce carbon dioxide. People and other animals breathe out the carbon dioxide they make. Plants take in more carbon dioxide than they produce. They use it in photosynthesis, the process in which they make their own food. Photosynthesis requires sunlight, chlorophyll (a substance in plants and certain algae), water, and carbon dioxide. It produces oxygen and carbon compounds called sugars, which plants use and store as food. People and other animals breathe in oxygen and depend on the sugars plants make for food.

This hippopotamus is eating a mouthful of river grass—both of which have tissues that contain carbon.

compareandcontrast

How are animals and plants similar? How are they different?

Humans and plants exchange carbon dioxide and oxygen and help each other survive.

Carbon in the Atmosphere

Earth's atmosphere has five layers and is made up of several gases. Near Earth's surface, the atmosphere is about three-fourths nitrogen and one-fifth oxygen. At higher elevations, the atmosphere is mostly hydrogen and helium.

Most of the carbon in the atmosphere is near Earth's surface.

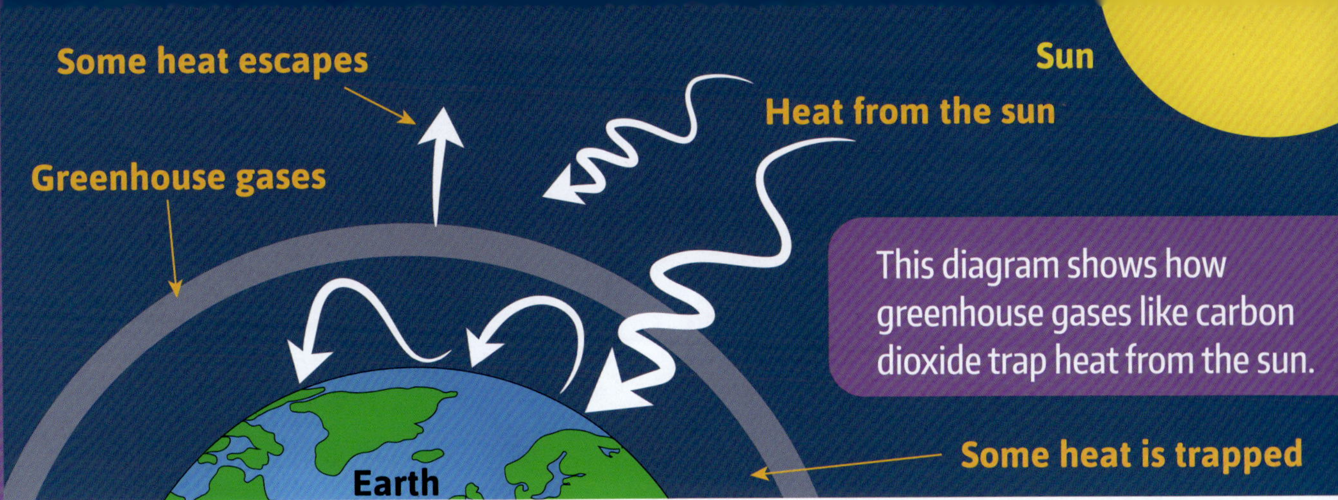

This diagram shows how greenhouse gases like carbon dioxide trap heat from the sun.

The atmosphere does not contain pure carbon, but it does have carbon dioxide and methane. Methane is another compound that contains carbon. Carbon dioxide and methane enter the atmosphere by things people do and by natural processes.

Carbon dioxide and methane are both greenhouse gases. They are called this because they keep heat in a certain area, like a greenhouse does. Land, oceans, and plants absorb, or soak up, energy from sunlight. They release some of this energy as heat. Greenhouse gases absorb the heat and then send it back toward Earth. This is called the greenhouse effect. Without greenhouse gases, this heat would escape back into space. Earth would be too cold for life to exist.

Consider This

Where does the heat that greenhouse gases trap come from?

Carbon in the Oceans

Earth's hydrosphere is made up of oceans and other bodies of water. The oceans are important carbon reservoirs. They keep much more carbon than they give out. In the carbon cycle, carbon has a long stay in the oceans.

There is far more carbon dioxide stored in deeper waters than on the ocean's surface.

A coral's skeleton is almost pure calcium carbonate.

Carbon is found in several forms in an ocean. Carbon dioxide from the atmosphere dissolves into the surface waters. Tiny ocean **organisms** called phytoplankton use the carbon dioxide in the water for photosynthesis. Other sea creatures eat phytoplankton. Their bodies combine carbon from the phytoplankton with calcium to make calcium carbonate. This white, powdery compound makes up the shells and skeletons of many ocean animals.

Most of the carbon in the ocean is found in deep water. When a sea creature dies, its body sinks to the bottom. The body decays, or breaks down, and carbon from the body tissue is released. The bits of carbon, with other materials, form layers that become rock over a long period of time.

WORD WISE

ORGANISMS ARE LIVING THINGS. ANIMALS, PLANTS, FUNGI, AND ALGAE ARE ALL ORGANISMS.

Carbon in the Earth

Carbon is found in abundance in the rocks and minerals of Earth's lithosphere. Rocks do not use the carbon like living things do. Carbon is stored in the rock. The two main forms of pure carbon in rocks are the minerals diamond and graphite. However, most of the carbon in rocks is in the form of carbon compounds.

Fossil fuels, which are buried in the lithosphere, are another carbon reservoir. Fossil fuels are the remains of organisms that lived long ago. When plants and animals die, their remains slowly decay. Eventually, they become buried under layers of soil. Over millions of years, they change to form different kinds of fossil fuels. Petroleum and natural gas come mainly from microscopic organisms such as algae. Coal comes from plants.

About 99.9 percent of all near-surface carbon is stored in Earth's rocks.

compareandcontrast

How is coal like other fossil fuels, such as petroleum and natural gas? How is it different?

The coal we burn for heat today took about 300 to 400 million years to form.

The Slow Cycle

The carbon that is stored in rock is part of the geological carbon cycle. This is also called the slow carbon cycle, because it can take hundreds of millions of years for carbon to complete the cycle.

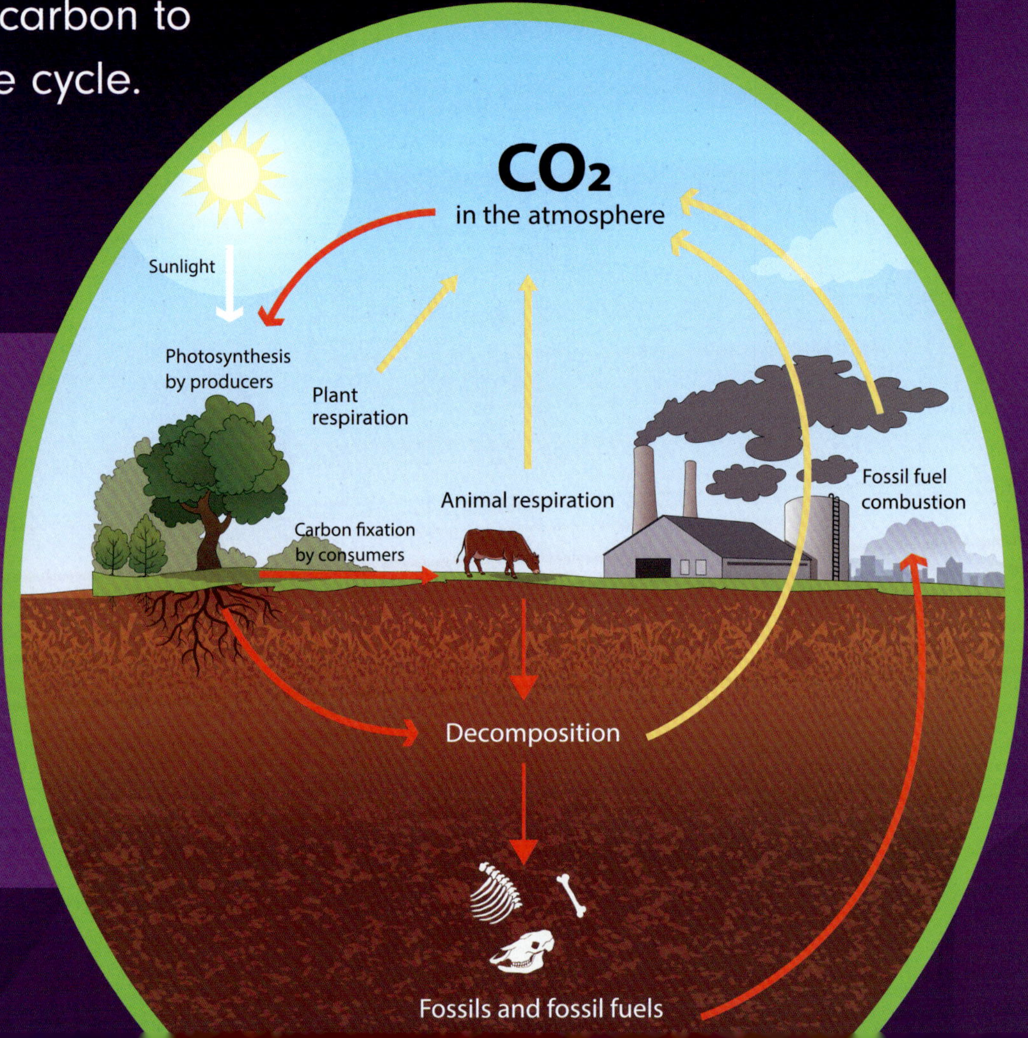

It takes millions of years for carbon trapped in fossil fuels to be released into the atmosphere.

The formations in this cave grew over the course of millions of years as water with calcium carbonate slowly dripped and hardened into rock.

In the atmosphere, carbon combines with water vapor to form a kind of acid. The acid falls to Earth in rain. On the ground, the acid dissolves rock very slowly. This process, called chemical weathering, releases elements, like calcium, from the rock. These elements are carried to the ocean by running water.

The bodies of some sea animals combine the calcium in the ocean with the carbon they get from eating plants. That forms the calcium carbonate that makes up their shells. When the animals die, their bodies sink to the bottom. As they layer and decay, a type of rock called **sedimentary** rock is formed. Carbon remains trapped in sedimentary rock until it is disturbed or removed.

WORD WISE

SEDIMENTARY ROCK IS PRODUCED WHEN DIRT AND DUST, CALLED SEDIMENT, ARE PRESSED TOGETHER TO MAKE ROCK.

The crust of Earth is not one solid layer. It is broken up into many pieces, called plates. Plates meet in many different locations on Earth, on land and in the ocean. Because the plates are constantly moving, rock is being pushed under other layers of rock all the time.

These pinnacle rock formations are made of weathered limestone (calcium carbonate). They are located in the Gunung Mulu National Park on the island of Borneo.

Karymsky volcano, located on the Kamchatka Peninsula in Russia, has been continuously erupting since 2001. Imagine all the carbon dioxide it has released into the atmosphere!

Pressure builds when plates move this way, and the result is a volcanic eruption. A volcano releases lava, or hot liquid rock, that cools and hardens on Earth's surface. It also releases millions of tons of carbon dioxide back into the atmosphere. From there, the cycle begins again.

Scientists think that the floor of the ocean spreads over time, pushing rock at the bottom of the ocean toward dry land. This process takes millions of years.

Consider This

How do the plates of Earth's crust affect volcanic eruptions?

The Fast Cycle

The biological carbon cycle is also called the fast carbon cycle. Carbon moves around the biosphere much more quickly than it moves through the geological carbon cycle.

Living things get the energy they need from a process called respiration. This process happens in the cells, so it is also called cellular respiration. Most living things—including plants and animals—need oxygen for respiration. They also need a simple sugar, called glucose. Plants (and some kinds of algae) make oxygen and glucose during photosynthesis. Animals breathe in oxygen from the air and get glucose from the foods they eat. Cellular respiration takes place when cells take in oxygen and sugar and release water and carbon dioxide. During this process, energy is also released.

Animals breathe out the carbon dioxide that was released from their cells. Plants take in carbon dioxide from the air to use in photosynthesis. The process of photosynthesis produces glucose, which is used by animals. And the biological carbon cycle continues.

When you blow bubbles, you are filling the soap bubbles with carbon dioxide from your lungs. You are contributing to the fast carbon cycle!

compare**and**contrast

How are the fast carbon cycle and the slow carbon cycle similar? How are they different?

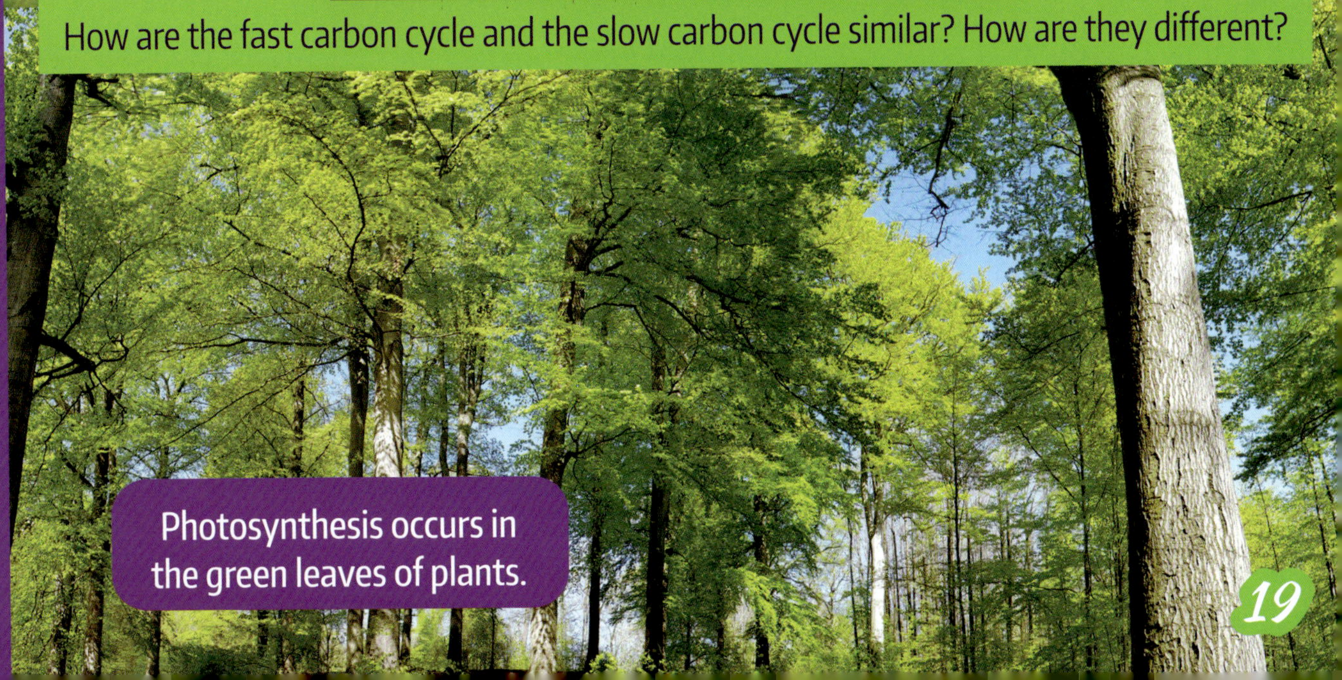

Photosynthesis occurs in the green leaves of plants.

Affecting the Atmosphere

Human actions can have a lasting effect on the carbon cycle. By breathing out, we help keep the cycle moving. However, other actions can have negative effects on the cycle.

Deforestation is the clearing of large areas of trees to create land for farming and building. When there are fewer plants to absorb carbon dioxide, more of the gas will stay in the atmosphere.

China, the United States, and India release the most carbon dioxide per year into the atmosphere. The main causes are electricity generation, industrial processes, and transportation.

When people burn fossil fuels, the process releases carbon that had been stored deep inside Earth. Cutting down trees (for wood or to make room for homes and businesses) means there are fewer trees to take in carbon dioxide. This leads to more carbon dioxide in the atmosphere.

More carbon dioxide in the atmosphere means that more heat gets trapped near Earth. Without human activity, Earth does a good job of balancing the amount of carbon that moves through the cycle. Since humans started adding carbon dioxide to the atmosphere, Earth's surface temperatures have begun to slowly rise.

Consider This

Which do you think absorbs more carbon dioxide—farms or forests? Why?

Affecting Land

Plants adjust how they grow as the planet's surface gets warmer. Warmer temperatures mean a longer growing season. That means that more food can be produced for humans and other animals. Scientists have discovered that plants are actually absorbing more carbon dioxide than they have in the past. This is called carbon fertilization.

Scientists take frequent samples to monitor the amount of carbon dioxide in farmland soil.

Dried soil makes it hard for plants to grow. So does soil that has few nutrients left in it.

It sounds like more plant growth is a good thing, but there are some problems. Plants don't just use carbon dioxide to grow. They also need water and nutrients like nitrogen from the soil. When a plant uses more carbon dioxide, it also uses more water and nutrients. This can dry out the soil in which the plant grows. The lack of nutrients and dry soil leads to poor plant growth.

Consider This

Why does more carbon dioxide in the atmosphere only cause a temporary increase in plant growth?

Affecting Oceans

Many marine organisms living in the hydrosphere are affected by any changes in the water. The extra heat trapped near Earth by extra carbon dioxide in the atmosphere makes for warmer waters, too. Warmer oceans increase the growth of some organisms and make it harder for others to survive.

Warming oceans can result in the lack of algae, which is corals' main food source. Weak from little food, the corals turn white. This is called coral bleaching.

Grinnell Glacier is located in Glacier National Park in Montana. These photographs, taken between 1938 and 2021, show how much ice has melted in recent years.

Extra carbon dioxide dissolved in the water makes the ocean more acidic. One effect of this is that animals have a harder time making their shells. Shells are a type of protection for these animals, so they are more likely to die if they have weak shells.

A rise in air and water temperatures also causes glaciers and sea ice to melt, which makes the water level of the ocean rise. As the water level rises, more land on the shores is covered with water.

Consider This

As sea levels rise, more of Earth's land will get covered with water. How do you think this will affect people who live on islands and coasts?

What Is Climate Change?

The gradual warming of Earth's air and waters is called climate change. To understand how our planet's climate has changed, the scientists must first search for clues about what the climate was like in the past. Scientists study how extra carbon dioxide in the atmosphere affects our planet.

Scientists study melting glacier water in Antarctica to determine the level of carbon dioxide in it.

Climate scientists use the newest technology to study warming patterns all over the world.

They can look at layers of rock for clues. The oldest layers are deep inside Earth. Scientists can also study gas bubbles in glaciers and the rings found in older trees. They also look for patterns by studying weather information that has been gathered over time.

Scientists have found that, throughout Earth's past, temperatures have gone up and down at different times. Some people think that this proves that human activity does not have much of an effect on climate. However, scientists say that the climate is changing much more quickly than it did in the past, and it's likely to continue for years to come.

Consider This

How will warming temperatures affect living things on Earth?

Protecting the Planet

People use coal, oil, and natural gas to run power plants, machines in factories, and cars. Fossil fuels make some things in our lives easier. However, burning fossil fuels can also be harmful to Earth. This can make our lives more difficult.

Burning coal is bad for the environment, but the mining process itself is as well.

Solar panels like these can help people reduce the amount of fossil fuels we burn.

Reducing our use of fossil fuels is a good idea for several reasons. When less fossil fuels are burned, less carbon dioxide is released into the air. Also, removing fossil fuels from the ground causes pollution and can be dangerous. Finally, the fossil fuels buried in Earth are nonrenewable, which means that they can be used up.

Using renewable sources of energy (or energy that does not run out) can help reduce the amount of carbon we take from the ground and release into the air. **Solar energy** and wind power are two types of renewable power sources that are being used more and more.

WORD WISE

SOLAR ENERGY IS ENERGY FROM THE SUN. SOLAR PANELS COLLECT THE SUN'S RAYS AND CHANGE IT INTO ELECTRICITY THAT CAN BE STORED IN BATTERIES.

Glossary

acidic Having a chemical that can break down substances.

algae Plantlike organisms, such as seaweed, that grow in water.

atom One of the tiny particles that are the building blocks of all matter.

chemical A basic substance that reacts with other substances in a predictable way.

compound Something made up of two or more elements.

decay To rot, decompose, or break down.

dissolve To evenly mix with one or more other substances.

element A natural substance that cannot be broken down into other substances.

microscopic Too small to be seen without a microscope.

mineral A chemical element or compound that results from natural, nonliving processes. Rocks are made of minerals.

nutrient A substance that helps living things grow.

photosynthesis The process by which green plants use sunlight to make their own food.

phytoplankton Tiny organisms that live in water and can make their own food using photosynthesis. Phytoplankton are mostly algae.

reservoir A place where something is stored or exists in large amounts.

respiration The process that takes place in the cells of all living things that creates the energy needed to live.

tissue A group of cells that work together to perform a function.

For More Information

Books

Becker, Trudy. *Glacier National Park*. Mendota Heights, MN: North Star Editions, 2025.

Hunt, Ian. *Climate Action for Kids: An Introduction to Climate Change*. Cambridge, MN: Adventure Publications, 2026.

Websites

Carbon Cycle Facts for Kids
kids.kiddle.co/Carbon_cycle
Read more about Earth's carbon cycle here.

Fossil Fuels Explained to Kids
kids.earth.org/climate-change/fossil-fuels-explained-to-kids
Learn more about fossil fuels and how burning them affects Earth.

Index